SHADOWS

by Meg Gaertner

Cody Koala

An Imprint of Pop!
popbooksonline.com

abdobooks.com
Published by Pop!, a division of ABDO, PO Box 398166, Minneapolis, Minnesota 55439. Copyright © 2020 by POP, LLC. International copyrights reserved in all countries. No part of this book may be reproduced in any form without written permission from the publisher. Pop!™ is a trademark and logo of POP, LLC.

Printed in the United States of America, North Mankato, Minnesota

052019
092019

THIS BOOK CONTAINS RECYCLED MATERIALS

Cover Photo: iStockphoto
Interior Photos: iStockphoto, 1, 7 (bottom left), 7 (bottom right), 9 (flashlight), 9 (ball), 11, 13, 14, 15, 19, 20–21; Shutterstock Images, 5, 7 (top); GIPhotoStock/ Science Source, 16–17

Editor: Connor Stratton
Series Designer: Sarah Taplin

Library of Congress Control Number: 2018964779
Publisher's Cataloging-in-Publication Data
Names: Gaertner, Meg, author.
Title: Shadows / by Meg Gaertner.
Description: Minneapolis, Minnesota : Pop!, 2020 | Series: Science all around | Includes online resources and index.
Identifiers: ISBN 9781532163616 (lib. bdg.) | ISBN 9781532165054 (ebook)
Subjects: LCSH: Shadows--Juvenile literature. | Light and darkness-- Juvenile literature. | Science--Juvenile literature.
Classification: DDC 535.4--dc23

Hello! My name is

Cody Koala

Pop open this book and you'll find QR codes like this one, loaded with information, so you can learn even more!

Scan this code* and others like it while you read, or visit the website below to make this book pop.

popbooksonline.com/shadows

*Scanning QR codes requires a web-enabled smart device with a QR code reader app and a camera.

Table of Contents

Chapter 1

What Is a Shadow?

A girl walks outside. A dark figure follows. It moves when she moves. It stops when she stops. It is her shadow. Shadows form when **opaque** objects block light.

Watch a video here!

Chapter 2

Light

Light shines from a **source**. This source could be the sun, a lamp, or a flashlight. Light shoots out in straight lines. These lines **beam** in all directions.

Complete an activity here!

The light hits an object.

The light cannot pass

through it. A dark spot

appears behind the object.

This spot is a shadow.

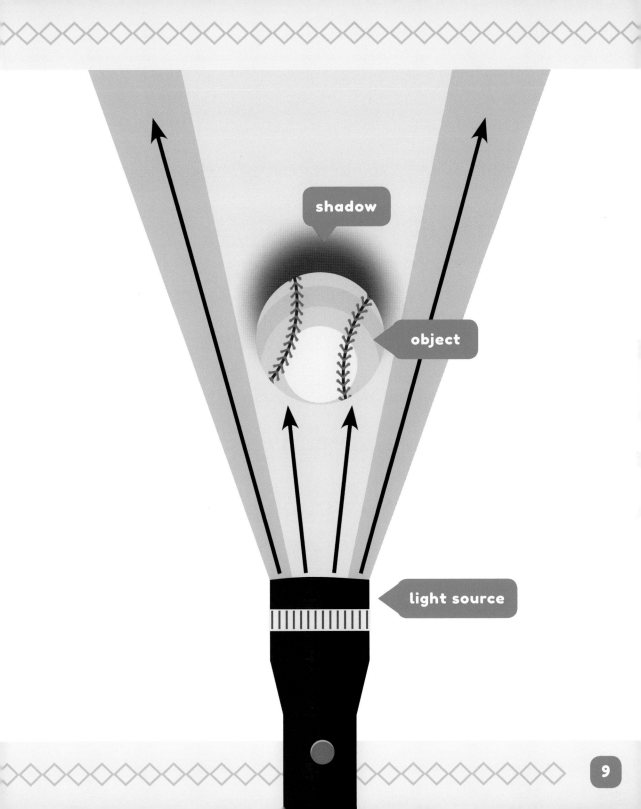

Not all objects have shadows. Some objects are **transparent**. They let all light through. Other objects are **translucent**. They let only some light through.

Translucent objects have fuzzy shadows.

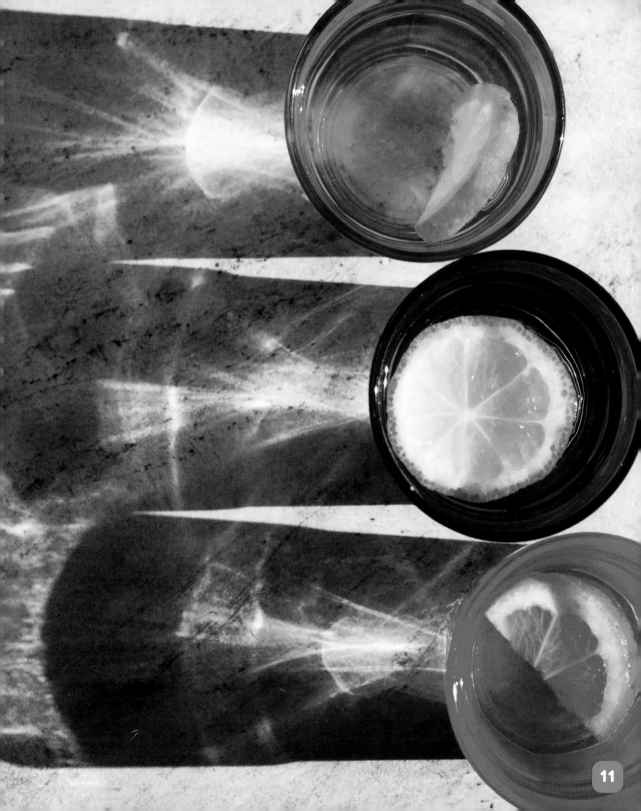

Chapter 3

Growing and Shrinking

Shadows change shape when their light **source** moves. The sun causes shadows to change throughout the day.

Learn more here!

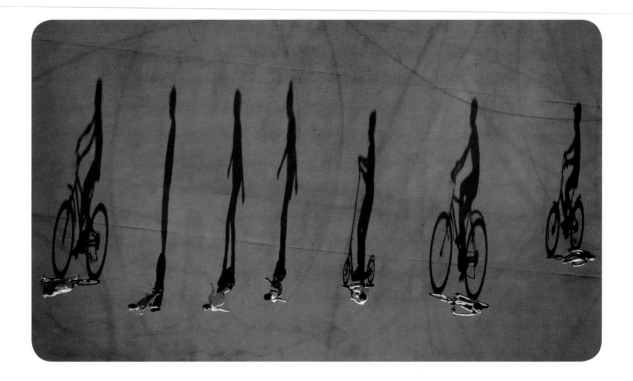

In the morning, the sun
is low in the sky. Objects
block more of the sun's
light. Shadows are long.

At noon, the sun is high in the sky. Objects block less of the sun's light. Shadows are short.

Shadows also change
when objects move. Move
an object away from a light.

light source

The shadow gets smaller.
Move the object close to the
light. The shadow grows.

Chapter 4

Useful Shadows

Shadows stay cool even on hot days. The sun's light makes heat. But shadows have less light, so they get less heat.

People used to tell time by watching shadows made by the sun.

Learn more here!

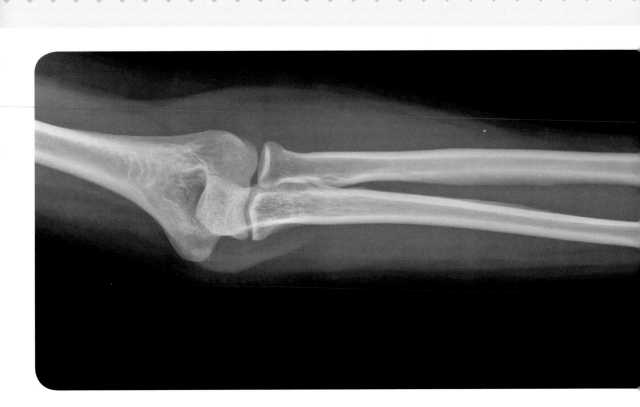

X-rays use shadows.

Doctors shine these rays

on a sick person. These

X-rays pass through skin.

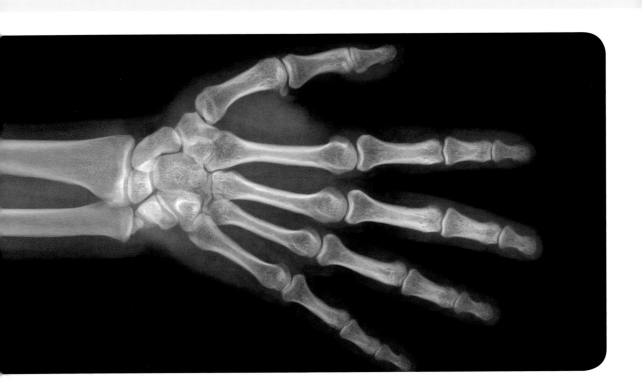

But they can't pass through
bone. Doctors look at
the shadow to see what
is wrong.

Making Connections

Text-to-Self

Where have you seen your shadow? What was the source of the light?

Text-to-Text

Have you read other books about light and shadows? What did you learn?

Text-to-World

Light cannot pass through opaque objects. It can pass through transparent objects. Look at the objects around you. Which are opaque? Which are transparent?

Glossary

beam – to send out a ray of light.

opaque – solid; not letting any light pass through.

source – the place that something else came from; the starting point.

translucent – allowing some, but not all, light to pass through.

transparent – clear; letting all light pass through.

X-ray – an image that lets doctors see inside a body without cutting it open.

Index

Online Resources

popbooksonline.com

Thanks for reading this Cody Koala book!

Scan this code* and others like it in this book, or visit the website below to make this book pop!

popbooksonline.com/shadows

*Scanning QR codes requires a web-enabled smart device with a QR code reader app and a camera.